ELEPHANTS NEVER FORGET

To my nieces and nephews: May you learn to let go of the things that weigh you down and hold onto the things that lift you up.

– Venita

For Clare and Coral, because I'll never forget.

– Natashia

Mini & Milo: Elephants Never Forget
first published in 2025
by Walker Books Australia Pty Ltd
Locked Bag 22, Newtown
NSW 2042 Australia
www.walkerbooks.com.au

This edition published in 2025.

Walker Books Australia acknowledges the Traditional Owners of the country on which we work, the Gadigal and Wangal peoples of the Eora Nation, and recognises their continuing connection to the land, waters and culture. We pay our respect to their Elders past and present.

A catalogue record for this book is available from the National Library of Australia

ISBN: 978 1 761601 88 0

The illustrations for this book were created digitally
Typeset in Ovo, with Blue Sheep, Bokka and Nippon Note
Printed and bound in China

EU Authorized Representative: HackettFlynn Ltd,
36 Cloch Choirneal, Balrothery, Co. Dublin, K32 C942, Ireland.
EU@walkerpublishinggroup.com

10 9 8 7 6 5 4 3 2 1

ELEPHANTS NEVER FORGET

Venita Dimos & Natashia Curtin

WALKER BOOKS
AND SUBSIDIARIES
LONDON • BOSTON • SYDNEY • AUCKLAND

Mini had the **best** memory in the whole, entire, animal kingdom. She remembered good stuff, bad stuff and **everything** in between.

Mini remembered phone numbers, passwords, places and faces. She even remembered things that happened **millions** of years ago.

'The Stegosaurus was the dinosaur with the smallest brain,' said Mini to her best friend, Milo.

Milo could **never** remember as much as Mini, but he **always** remembered his manners.

But because Mini remembered **everything**, she also remembered **Mistakes**. Usually other people's mistakes.

Big Mistakes,

small mistakes,

funny mistakes ...

and especially

Milo's Mistakes.

'Remember the time you **lost** my favourite bouncy ball?'

'Remember the time you **broke** my special pink pencil?'

‘Remember the time you **copied** my rainbow painting?’

‘I wish you **could** forget sometimes, Mini!’ said Milo.

But Mini was **proud** of her excellent memory. It made her feel **special** and **smart**.

One morning, Milo was practising one of his **Magic** tricks, with the assistance of Mini's snuggly toy, Mr Cuddles.

'And now, I'm going to make Mr Cuddles **disappear!**' Milo announced.

When Milo and Mini peered inside the magic hat, Mr Cuddles **wasn't there**.

'Hooray!' said Mini.

Milo took a bow.

'And now, I'm going to make Mr Cuddles come back!' said Milo.

'Abracadabra!'

Milo and Mini peered inside the magic hat. But Mr Cuddles ... **still** wasn't there!

‘Where’s Mr Cuddles?’ said Mini.

‘Hmmm,’ said Milo, tapping his magic hat one more time.

Milo and Mini looked inside the hat,

but Milo really **had** made Mr Cuddles **disappear**.

'Bring him **BACK!**' said Mini.

'Oh no, Mini!' said Milo. 'I must have made a **MISTAKE!**'

'A BIG MISTAKE!' Mini yelled. 'And I will **NEVER** forget it!'

The next morning, Milo brought Mini a **brand-new** Mr Cuddles.

'That's not Mr Cuddles. He's the wrong shape,' said Mini.

Milo tried another new Mr Cuddles.

'That's not Mr Cuddles either,' said Mini.

Milo made Mini a daisy chain and an **enormous** 'sorry' cake.
Mini tried to smile, but the big mistake was **still** there.

'Sorry Milo,' said Mini. 'I **can't** forget.'

For the rest of that day, the **BIG** mistake **flipped** and **tossed** in Mini's head. Everywhere she went, the **BIG** mistake followed. The **BIG** mistake kept Mini awake **all night**.

Mini decided that she **should** forget Milo's mistake.

But she didn't know how to **not** remember it.

But she also knew she **had** to try.

She tried reading a book.
But that didn't work.

She tried watching TV.
That didn't work either.

She tried playing some games ...
but still, nothing worked.

And **none** of it was any fun
without Milo.

Mini sighed. She couldn't find a way to stop remembering **everything**, even her **own mistakes**.

Like when she **sat** on George.

And the time she **broke** the see-saw.

And when she accidentally **let go** of her balloon, and it floated up in the sky ...

gone **forever.**

That was it!

Maybe Mini could find a way for the big mistake to float away ... just like her balloon.

The next day Mini met Milo in the park. She was carrying a big red balloon.

'What's that for?' said Milo.

'You'll see,' said Mini.

'**IMagine** the balloon is the big mistake,' said Mini.

'Okay,' said Milo, confused.

'It's time to let the big mistake go,' said Mini, letting go of the balloon.

Mini and Milo watched as the red balloon soared ...

up

up

up higher and higher …

Soon, all Mini and Milo could see was a little red dot on the horizon. And then it … **disappeared.**

'Good-bye big Mistake!' said Mini.

'Good-bye big Mistake!' said Milo.

The next day, Mini felt better without the big mistake following her around.

And Mini's mum suggested they spend the day learning how to make things **appear.**

'Mr cuddles
you're back!'

Mini learned that sometimes you **can let things go**, even if you **can't** forget.

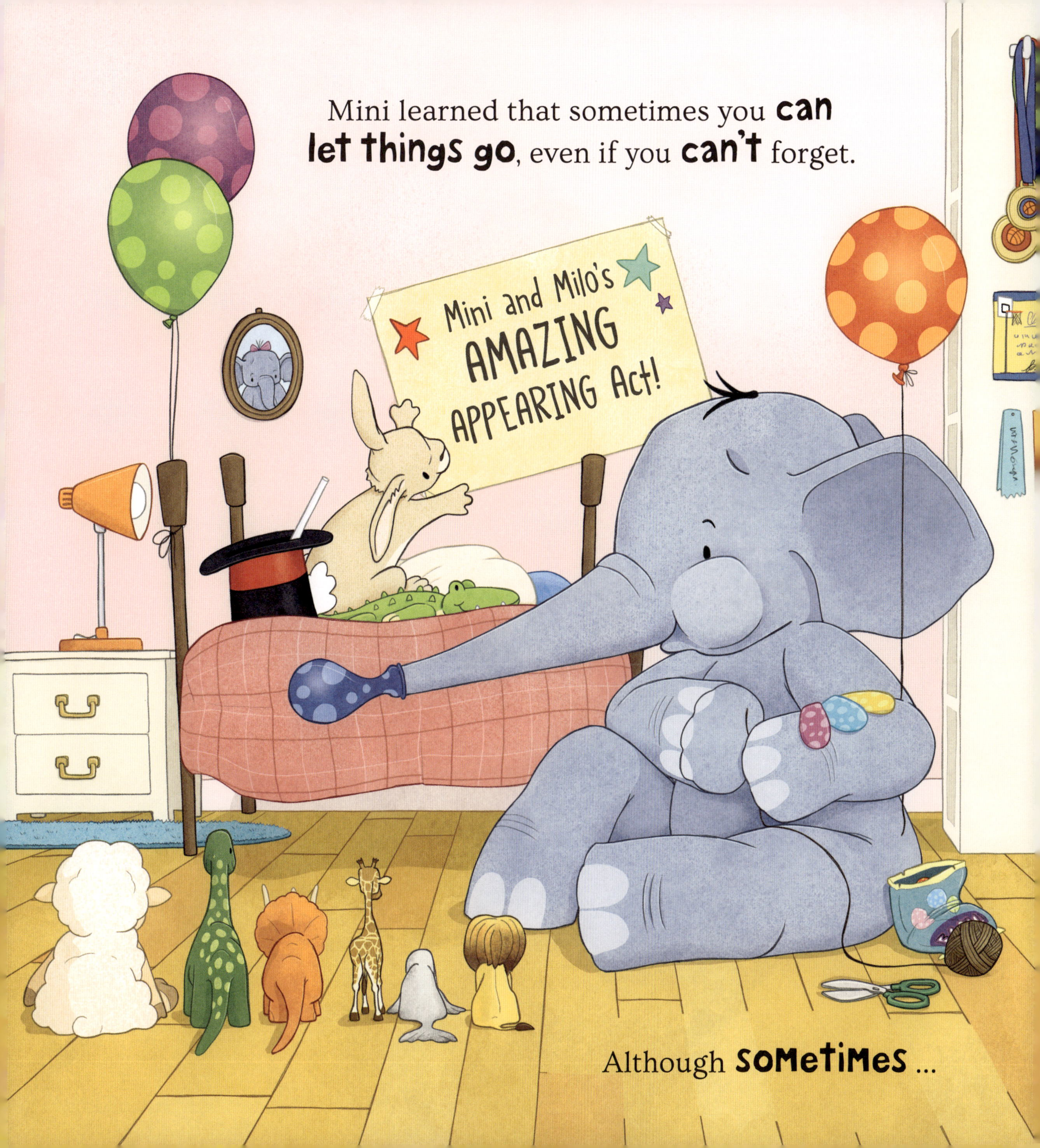

Although **sometimes** ...

‘Milo, remember three years ago when you lost my favourite bouncy ball?’